Getting started in Junior Dragster racing: a beginners guide.

By Richard Crichton

Contents

About this book 4

What is Junior Dragster racing? 6

What do you need to go Junior Dragster racing. 11

Racing cars, equipment and choices 29

Safety Equipment 30

    Helmets and neck restraints. 31

    Fire suits. 35

    Boots and gloves. 36

Renting, buying and building cars. 38

Tyres and tyre pressures 47

Engines 51

How the engine works 54

Junior dragster engines explained 59

    Piston rings 60

    Connecting Rod 62

    Piston 63

    Cylinder Head 64

    Flywheels and coils 65

    Carburettors 67

    Fuel pumps 69

    Clutches 70

Slowing cars down. 75
    Ballast 75
    Air restrictors 77
    Throttle stops..78
    Timing 79
    Gearing...80
Data Recorders 82
Qualification and competition. 84
Setting dial in times. 91
Winning races 93
The games people play 100
Troubleshooting..108

About this book

Back when we started out in junior dragster I looked through articles on the internet and talked to a few people that were already racing. There didn't seem to be a real book or manual on how you go about it, what you need to know, what to do, what to buy etc. It seemed pretty frustrating trying to find out anything and I thought back then that I should write a guide book, but obviously I didn't know anything then, but now, after some event wins, lots of round wins and several years' experience, both good and bad, it seems like I have amassed enough knowledge to at least pass on the basics to anyone thinking of starting out. This is an unashamedly "real" view of the class and how to get along in it.

Since we first started in the class in a rented Junior Stock car, through to our final season in a 90mph JMA we have seen and solved a lot of problems, issues and technical difficulties, but just when you think you have seen everything that a junior dragster can throw at you, another issue pops up to make you scratch your head and wonder how to solve. These are the things that have made the class such a joy for us over the years and some have been explained in this book. I hope as the reader you can gain something from reading this, but it is only intended to be a rough guide. Each and every reader will have their own experiences through the sport and I hope you all go on to enjoy it as much as we have.

What is Junior Dragster racing?

FUN! At its heart, the class is a 660ft (201m) lawnmower powered race for children. It is the entry level and training school for the full size classes and is an enjoyable experience in the family friendly, low cost (relative to other motorsports), exciting sport of drag racing. Fundamentally a drag race is an acceleration contest between two vehicles over a measured distance. The distance raced in junior dragster is 1/8 mile (660 ft.) whilst most of the rest of the sport races over 1/4 mile (1320 ft.). In its organised format, drag racing has a large number of specific classifications, each of which will have its own class rules and regulations. There are three basic ways in which a race is organised, junior dragster run as a bracket class, where all the entrants compete against each other and the performance differences between faster and slower vehicles is removed by a handicap delay in the starting system. Other classes such as Super Gas run as an index class, where the idea is to get as close to the class index as possible, each of the index classes run to a different time index. Super Street run to the 10.90 index, with Super Gas running to 9.90 and Super Comp, the quickest at 8.90. The first time racer may struggle with the concept of running to an index, after all, isn't drag racing about going as fast as you can? Once you have visited the track a few times though, you will understand that making a car run an exact time is equally as difficult as making it go the quickest possible. Professional classes including Top Fuel and Pro Mod run their races with no bracket or index, in a method of racing called "heads up". The main thing to remember about drag racing is that it is the most simple of motorsports, made incredibly complex by the people who do it! There is always a lot of talk up and down the pit lane about tactics and methods, gamesmanship and strategy. As a beginner, and, I would say, all the way through your drag racing career, the most important thing to remember is that whilst there is usually a car in the other lane, the only person that you really have to race is yourself. If you can just remember that every time you approach the line, your experience in the sport will be much happier.

Junior Dragster racing is the training class for the drivers of the future; racers may begin their career at 8 years old and finish at 18. In between these ages, racers progress through a number of stages within the class. At the time of writing, a junior dragster driver begins their career at 8 years old in a class called Junior Stock (JS). These cars are built to the same dimensions as the more senior cars but are powered by 100cc-200cc motors, usually fuelled by petrol and producing something in the region of 8-15 hp. A JS car is limited to a time of 11.90 seconds with terminal speeds in the region of 40mph. This may sound pretty slow when compared to the older drivers cars, but as an 8 year old it is plenty quick enough to begin your career. We must consider that this is an acceleration contest and so a JS car will get up to speed over 1/8 mile which is just 200m. The world record for sprinting that distance is around 19 seconds, so a JS driver is out accelerating Usain Bolt! Once the child is 10 years old they can progress to Junior Modified (JM). These cars are the same chassis as the JS cars, but are allowed to run with a larger displacement motor, running on methanol and producing around 25-30hp. JM cars are limited to 8.90 seconds for the $1/8^{th}$ mile which will often see them crossing the finish line at between 60 and 70 mph. At the age of 13 the driver can progress to Junior Modified Advanced (JMA) which again have allowances for increased displacement engines, but also now require a chassis constructed from Chrome moly. These cars allow competitors to race down to 7.90 seconds for the 1/8th and terminal speeds of up to 85mph. It is possible to start a Junior Dragster career at any stage between 8 and 18, and it is also possible to drive the same chassis for your entire career if the car is selected well initially. Engines will need to be upgraded, but it is possible to race on just one engine throughout a JM and JMA career. It is also technically feasible to race on just one block from JS to JMA, though this is much more complicated and will be discussed later on.

The whole purpose and ethos of Junior Dragster racing is to provide race craft training to the racers of the future. In theory and in practice it is possible to commence ones senior drag racing career at the age of 16, before it is even possible to drive a road car in many countries. The idea that a 16 year old could begin racing in a vehicle with many more horsepower than a standard road car is frightening enough in itself, but that this could happen without the driver being aware of the protocols and practicalities of a drag race is beyond credible. For this reason the governing bodies of drag racing in New Zealand proposed and introduced the class back in 1988 with the NHRA in America following on in 1991. The first junior dragsters in Europe started to race in the late 1990's. Full championships operate in all the sanctioning bodies across the world nowadays and large fields of cars compete in championship events.

What do you need to go Junior Dragster racing.

In simple terms, you need to be able bodied enough to control a car, you need to be over 8 years old (at the time of writing, though this may drop to 5 years old). After those two obstacles have been passed, all you need is a car, which you can rent from most tracks to get you started, a licence, which is applied for via your track and your national association, the requisite safety equipment and an event to race at. If you are going to continue racing more than just a couple of events, you will probably want your own car, but you can genuinely start your racing career for a very reasonable amount of money. The choices for buying or building a car will be dealt with in a later chapter, but for now we will assume that you have rented a car and been provided with the relevant safety equipment as part of that rental. In this opening section we will look at the actual process of racing, what everything means and why.

Drag races take place on a prepared track with (usually) two side by side measured lanes. The lanes are a quarter of a mile long and are sub divided by light beams into shorter sections of 60 feet, 330 feet, 594 feet, 660 feet (an $1/8^{th}$ of a mile and the finish line for junior dragsters) 1000 feet, 1254 feet and 1320 feet (1/4 of a mile - finish line for the senior classes). Each of these light beams is triggered when a vehicle crosses them. Breaking a beam allows a computer in race control to calculate the time taken for a vehicle to travel from the start line to the location of the light beam and therefore can calculate the speed and elapsed time of that vehicle. Drag racers talk about two different measurements; Elapsed time (ET) is the total amount of time taken to travel over any or all the segments of the track. Terminal speed is the speed the vehicle was travelling when it crossed the finish line. Speeds are also measured and provided for each distance along the track.

Races are started by means of a light system called a Christmas tree, often just called the tree. This is a series of lights which have different purposes and require different treatment by the driver and the team. Since the tree is the most important element in the first stages of racing it is worth explaining the purpose of each of the lights and how they are controlled, activated and what they each mean, but first of all, there are a number of other officials, rules and details worth mentioning for the true beginner. Drag race events and races are held between vehicles of broadly equal performance. These are arranged into classes at a full event and each class will progress through their qualifications or eliminations together. The classes wait back in the pits until they are called. Call up methods vary between tracks and may be a person, a tannoy announcement or a communication through a radio station, mobile phone or other method. Whichever is the case at the track you are competing at, the call is made and you take your car and driver to a collecting area behind the start line where you wait your turn. Drivers should be seated in their cars wearing all their required safety equipment and with helmets on and secured and seatbelts locked and tightened before they approach the track. A track official will signal you to start your car when you get to the front of the queue. Your driver will then proceed under power out onto the track.

 There are a number of track officials on the start line who will have a look at the car and the driver as it makes its way to the start line, checking that requisite safety equipment is present and correctly worn or fitted, that the car is safe and not dropping any fluids or visibly dangerous. The track safety officials will indicate to the starter that the car is safe to compete. Assuming you have made it this far you are now ready to "take the tree"

In the centre of the tree there is a call up light which is activated by the timing crew to tell drivers that the start line is ready to receive a car or cars. On each side of the tree at the top there is a pre stage light, usually two orange bulbs. This light indicates that the car is approaching the line and nearing its start position. Below that are a second set of bulbs called the stage lights. These come on when a car is on the line. Both of these lights are controlled by light beams which run across the track. The front wheels of the car break the light beam and this causes the lighting circuit to switch on indicating to the driver that their car is in position. The beams should be approached and broken slowly and under full control so that the car does not pass through a beam too early and risk forfeiting the race.

There is a seven inch gap between the pre stage and the stage beams on the track. If your driver has staged perfectly then the pre stage lights should be on and the stage lights should flicker on at the same time. This would be perfectly staged, however occasionally you will see a car that has crept a little too far forwards and the pre stage beam has been re-made so the pre stage light goes off. If the stage light is still on, this is still OK, but the car is a little too far forwards and the next stage of the process becomes more difficult.

Once both the pre stage and stage lights are illuminated, the race is ready to commence. If the chief starter is happy that both drivers are ready to start and the race is safe to proceed, they will press the start system button. Once the button is pressed the starting sequence will commence after a short random delay. The sequence for Junior Dragsters is a series of three amber lights which are positioned in a vertical row on your side of the tree. The top amber will light up followed at half second intervals by the second and third amber lights. Another half a second later the green light comes on indicating that the race is underway. Whilst it is possible to wait until the green light is on before pulling away from the line, drag races are very often won or lost by the driver's reaction to the tree. The absolute ideal is to cross the start line just as the circuit for the green light is made. The difference between the point that the green lights up and the point where the stage beams are remade is called the reaction time or RT.

At this point it is also worth explaining the beams, their positions and their purpose. I have heard many people talking about racing who have obviously never worked out quite how a race is measured. Many people think that the clocks start when the green light comes on. This is not correct and an understanding of the process and sequence of events prior to the time clocks starting to record is worth having for the Junior Dragster parent and racer. This is knowledge that can win races if it is used correctly.

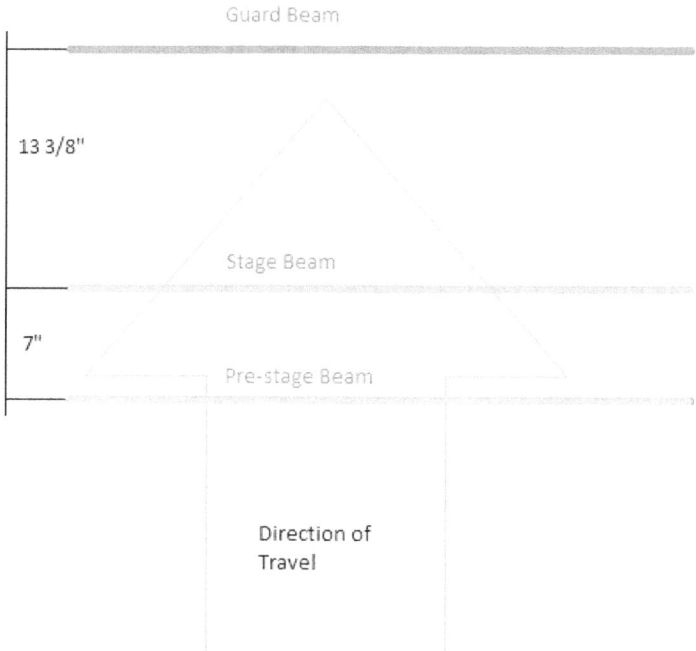

The pre stage beam is the first beam that a car crosses; this illuminates the pre-stage bulbs on the tree. A further 7 inches down the track there is the second beam, the stage beam. If you consider the shape of a wheel, it is obvious that if the beams were positioned at the right height, then the front edge of the wheel could have blocked the stage beam before the rear of the wheel has moved out of the way of the pre-stage beam, therefore we usually see the stage lights come on whilst the pre-stage lights are still illuminated. The timing system begins running the instant the stage beam is remade. A further 13 3/8 inches down the track from the stage beam is another light beam called the guard beam. This beam guards against false starts or interference with the stage beam by bodywork or chassis sections. If the guard beam is broken before the stage beam is remade, the start is deemed to be foul and the racers time is disqualified. The vehicle's wheel breaks the light beams when it moves in to stage, when the stage beam is re made as the vehicle moves away, the clocks start and the run timing begins. If we consider again the geometry of a wheel, it is clear that the stage beam can be broken by the leading edge of the wheel and remain broken until the whole of the wheel has passed through the beam location for it to be re-made.

This is referred to as the roll-out. The roll out is obviously affected by the height of the stage beam, track timing officials spend a great deal of time setting up timing systems such that they are always the same. This being the case, it is possible to understand the roll out of an individual car, and since we are trying to get off the line in the shortest possible time, especially in Junior Dragster classes, then understanding this can be crucial.

For every car there will be a small lag between the opening of the throttle and the delivery of power and acceleration to the rear wheels. This lag is unfortunately a variable and will be different under different weather conditions, but will remain within a range. Understanding this element of your car will give you a major advantage as the driver searches for the optimum position on the tree to hit the pedal.

Then we need to consider that dragsters are designed with offset front wheels, to allow for better staging, i.e. the leading edge of one of the front wheels is ahead of the leading edge of the other, which obviously means that the trailing edges differ by the same amount. This means that only the leading edge of one wheel has broken the stage beam, and we then have the distance from the leading edge to the trailing edge of that wheel plus the offset to the trailing edge of the other wheel as a distance to cover before the stage beam is re-made. The combination of these two factors means that to leave exactly when the green light illuminates, a driver has to have reacted in advance. If a driver hits the throttle pedal exactly as the green comes on, they will have a pretty poor (by drag racing standards) reaction time.

Just working on the geometry we can see that if the beams are sited at the regulation 2 inches above the track surface, and are set out at the regulation 7 inches distance between them, then a wheel of 16" diameter with a one inch tyre on it will have an overall diameter of 18" and a circumference of 56 ½ ". A horizontal line drawn through this wheel 2" above the ground has a span of around 12".

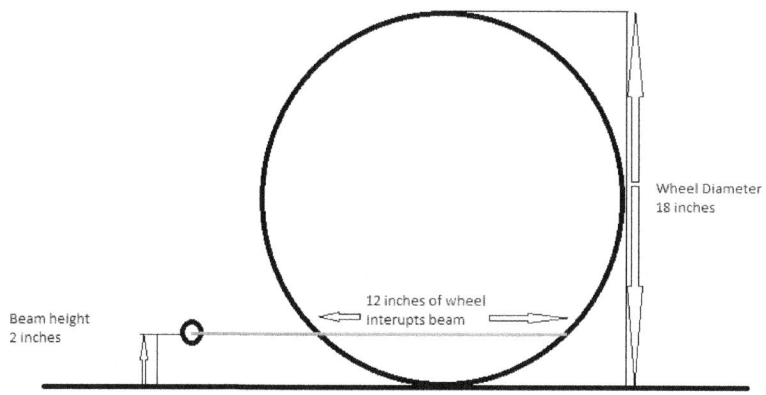

This is the distance that such a wheel must travel through before the beam is remade at the trailing edge. As mentioned previously there is an offset to the front wheels to help with staging and reaction times. This is not permitted to be greater than 2" in junior dragster classes, so a car with 16" rims and the maximum permissible offset has a maximum distance of just over 14" to travel from breaking, to remaking the stage beam. If drivers can train themselves to always sit at the same point in the stage beam, then they can learn to leave, pressing the accelerator at the optimum point such that the car is in motion and the stage beam is remade just as the green light comes on.

Achieving low reaction times is a core skill for the junior racer since this is the means by which qualification for events is decided. It is common for large fields of juniors to compete. In NHRA this could be numbered in the hundreds of cars but in Europe is usually between 20 and 30 cars. A high qualifying position is important as the rest of the competition is conducted against a knock out ladder which pits the upper half of the qualification order against the lower half.

At certain events there may also be a maximum number of competitors that will qualify for race day. If there are more entrants than race places, only those cars and drivers that qualify within the number of race places will get to race in eliminations. This is not terribly common in Junior Dragster racing where usually all entrants will get to race, but at larger events it can happen, so is worth being aware of. Drag races are conducted against eliminations ladders which naturally filter down to 2 cars for the final. This means that ladders are constructed with 4, 8, 16, 32 etc. qualification places on them. Any competition field (without a bump spot) is arranged for eliminations against the next highest number available for a whole ladder, i.e. 9 - 15 car fields would compete on a 16 car ladder. This obviously means that there will be spaces on the ladder which do not contain a car. These rounds are filled with "Bye runs" which indicate that no car competes. Bye runs are usually arranged as far as possible against each other so one bye run advances to the next round. In odd numbered fields, there is always a bye run in the first round for the number one qualifier. The rest of the bye runs will be paired off against each other and will filter back in against a competing car at later stages, often so that the number 2 qualifier would face a bye run, assuming they have stayed in the competition.

This is why it is important for a junior racer to learn the qualification process so that they are able to consistently qualify well. Additionally, in eliminations it is common for races to be won on the tree, and so a good start line procedure is imperative. The section on Qualifying and reaction times later in this book provides some well tested hints and tips on getting better reaction times.

 In eliminations, races are conducted against a "dial-in" which is the Elapsed Time in which the team believe the car will complete the $1/8^{th}$ mile. Setting your dial in is another key skill, and the only thing that will help (other than bucket loads of luck) is experience. The more a driver competes, tests and runs, the more information the team will have at their disposal to decide on a dial-in.

Junior dragsters race in eliminations against each other and therefore it is likely that quick and fast cars will have an elimination round against slower cars. Since a drag race is effectively a race to the line, these races need to be started such that the advantage of a fast car is eliminated from the competition. To achieve this, races are started individually per lane, which means in a race between a junior stock car that has dialled 13 seconds and a JMA car that has dialled 8 seconds, the stock car will leave the line 5 seconds before the JMA. It is then the job of the JMA to hunt down and pass the stock car but without going faster than 8 seconds. Completing the lap quicker than dial in is referred to as a break out and generally results in losing the round. The only time this is not the case is when the other car red lights, or breaks out by more. If we consider that the delay on the tree for the faster car, added to their dial in equals the dial in of the slower car, it is possible to understand how important a reaction time can be. If the JS car leaves the line with a perfect reaction time and the JMA leaves after 0.11 seconds, the JS can run one tenth slower than their dial in and still win the race even if the JMA runs to a perfect dial in.

As explained above, the clocks do not start running until the car leaves the line and so in a race to the finish line, a car that has started first has the advantage. It is fairly common to see racers run closer to their dial in than their opponent and yet still lose simply because their reaction time was slower.

Racing cars, equipment and choices

The choices for teams wishing to compete in junior dragster racing are varied and each has its own advantages and disadvantages. In this section I will give an overview of most of the common elements that go into any junior dragster team. This section is intended to help you understand the technical aspects of a junior dragster, it is not intended to recommend or promote any particular item, brand, choice or method. The final choices for your race team will be based on your own personal preferences, budgets and constraints. There is not a defined right and wrong way to go racing, other than the rule book with which you must comply, but other than the specific rules, choices are still wide and varied.

Safety Equipment

No matter how you choose to go racing, you will need to ensure your driver is correctly attired with regulation clothing. The most practical advice in this section is to always buy safety equipment from a known vendor. Too many times in racing forums and magazines we see articles, warnings and forum threads regarding fake or sub-standard safety equipment. Whether you are the parent, guardian, relative or the driver yourself you must agree that safety is paramount. From the smallest junior stock car to the quickest JMA and outlaw cars, every driver has taken the choice to strap themselves into a rapidly accelerating vehicle and launch themselves down a track. Whenever I am asked how I feel about the safety of my drivers, my answer is always the same. We are racing at a regulated track with qualified medics and fire fighters in attendance, race control and the start line crew are making sure that the track is in safe condition and there are only ever two cars on track at any one time. Accidents can still happen, regardless of the level of scrutiny and competence of the race officials and so the drivers are securely strapped into the cars with approved seatbelts, they are wearing fire safety equipment, approved crash helmets, fire protective gloves and boots and they are encased in a roll cage. Compromising on any level of this safety equipment is a ridiculous and extremely short sighted idea.

Helmets and neck restraints.

Helmets must meet a "type approval" rating specified by the governing body of the sport. In Europe, at the time of writing this standard is Snell 2010. These type approvals have a time limit and standards are upgraded periodically so it is worth checking with your race club, rule book and official body prior to purchasing a helmet so that the standard you buy is not going to be out of date within a few months. Helmets can be expensive, but it is not necessarily the case that the most expensive helmet is the best helmet. Fit and comfort are more important than the price. Always buy the best fitting crash helmet you can afford. The type approval for the helmet required will almost certainly mean that your choice is limited to only a handful of brands and shell designs. Selecting the one that fits best is a case of making sure it fits snuggly without pressing hard on any areas of the skull. Close fitting helmets should produce an element of "hamster cheeks" but should not be uncomfortably tight on any part of the head. A well fitted helmet should move with the head. This can be tested by holding the helmet still and asking the wearer to raise and lower their chin and turn their head from side to side. A helmet that fits is one that allows only a small amount of movement, no more than 1-2cm before it turns or raises and lowers with the child's head. It is important to remember that the internal padding in a new helmet will soften and collapse a little over time so a helmet that is tight today will loosen up after a weekends racing.

Helmets are designed to absorb impacts, and can only successfully achieve their purpose if they are looked after correctly; they should be cared for, stored and handled only in accordance with the manufacturer's instructions. Certain adhesives, paints and cleaning products can weaken the structure so only ever allow reputable persons to paint helmets and never attach stickers or decals to a helmet surface unless you are sure that they are suitable for this purpose. Helmets should be replaced if there has been any incident which may have cracked or damaged the shell such as dropping the helmet or allowing it to fall from shelves or tables. Cracks can be too small to see with the naked eye and it is really not worth finding out your helmet was damaged when you need it most, i.e. in an accident. For this reason I always advocate that helmets are kept as close to, if not on, floor level as possible. Too many times I have seen teams put helmets on the top of the roll cage or rear wing, and then watched them fall or be knocked onto the pavement.

When he was not wearing it, I always insisted my son's helmet was either on the floor or in the empty driver's seat where it was safe from incident.

Each driver must also wear a neck restraint device which could be in the form of a "donut" of foam that velcro's into position between the helmet chin bar and the shoulders and neck, or could be a full HANS (or similar) shoulder mounted device that attaches to the helmet via purpose made posts screwed into the helmet shell.

Neck restraints help to mitigate risk in an accident by stabilising and reducing the movement of the helmet. Helmets are relatively heavy which means that in an accident they can apply an additional force to the muscles and structures of the neck. A neck restraint is designed to cushion or limit the movement of the neck to minimise these forces.

At the time of writing HANS devices are not compulsory in junior dragsters however it is only a matter of time until a rule is passed which mandates the use of HANS devices for the class. Until that point, a neck restraint "donut" compliant with SFI 3.3 is sufficient.

It is important to understand that HANS devices (Head And Neck System) are built with varying degrees of rake. A driver that is sitting broadly upright in the car will need a lesser degree of rake than a driver that is ostensibly laying down in the car. Advice should be sought from a reputable vendor as to which HANS device is best suited to your particular set up. HANS devices attach to posts fitted to the helmet and are secured by the shoulder straps of the seat belts. Not all helmets are HANS compatible so it is important to match the device to the helmet.

Fire suits.
The minimum requirement for a fire suit in junior dragster is SFI 3.2A/1 (or FIA 1986/2000). This specification (or higher) must be clearly

labelled on any fire suit that you purchase. Many karting suits are not eligible for drag racing as they do not comply. Suits must cover the driver's body fully and may be of one or two piece design. SFI 3.2 is the specification for all approved race suits whether driving Formula One or Top Fuel Dragster. The A/1 suffix indicates an approximate time that the suit is capable of providing protection against second degree burns. Suits with a rating of A/1 have a burn protection time of greater than 3 seconds. Additionally they have a flame pass rating which is the time in which the fabric self-extinguishes of greater than 2 seconds. Particularly with smaller children the suit ranges available are limited to SFI 3.2 A/1, but increasingly suit manufacturers are providing higher ratings in more size ranges. As with helmets, it is always worth buying the best that you can afford.

Boots and gloves.

Race boots should be of primarily non-synthetic construction. Boots will protect driver's feet in the event of a crash and therefore must be at least ankle high to ensure that they remain on the foot, but they must also be flexible enough to allow operation of accelerator and brake without hindrance. There is no current minimum regulatory standard for boots in Junior Dragster, but they are available to SFI 3.3/5 which is a suitable standard.

Gloves must be non-synthetic and flame retardant. Gloves should be of gauntlet type construction with a wrist strap to secure them to the hand. There is no current mandatory standard for gloves in Junior dragster, but they are available in SFI3.3/1 standards and above which is a suitable standard.

Drivers must also use wrist restraints which are strap devices that join the wrists to the seatbelt to ensure that the driver's arms cannot come out of the cockpit in the event of a crash.

Renting, buying and building cars.

As I mentioned in the opening chapter, most tracks have at least one junior dragster that can be rented for events. In most cases these will be a JS car and this is likely to be the car in which you begin your career. Cars can be rented for test days and run what you brung days as well as full events. In order to enter a full event, a driver must be licenced to compete, so it is unlikely that you will be able to start your career in a points scoring event. The track will clearly set out their rental days and any restrictions which may apply when you contact them to arrange your hire. Once you have satisfied the track officials that you are competent in and around the car you can apply for the licence which will allow you to compete. Cars may be rented for events and may compete freely. Rented cars have won events before so the fact that this is not your own car is no barrier to racing. It is a relatively cheap way to build up experience and gain an entry point into the sport and serves also as useful time around other drivers and teams during which you can learn about other cars, other levels within the class and make decisions about whether the sport is for you and whether to buy a second hand car, a new fully built car or to build your own.

Since junior dragster racers compete from the ages of 8 to 18, there are always cars available to buy from drivers that have either moved up a level or are too old for the class. Before buying a car it is important to have a plan in mind for your future within the sport. If you plan to compete for a long time and to progress your car through JS to JMA, it is important to remember that a JMA car must be constructed from chrome moly tubing. Chrome moly is a type of steel alloyed with Chromium and Molybdenum. It is used in high strength applications because it exhibits better strength/weight characteristics than ordinary carbon steels. Like everything in engineering, there is always a compromise, and in the case of chrome moly steel this is the fact that it is more difficult to weld than ordinary carbon steel. Unless you are a proficient welder it is generally advisable to have any chrome moly chassis building and welding done by a reputable chassis builder. If you are new to racing, then simply asking around the pit lane will definitely throw up trusted names within your area.

Buying a second hand car has certain advantages. First it will come (usually) as a complete package with engine, wheels, tyres etc. Secondly the ex-owners will usually be only too happy to provide help and guidance, and thirdly, it will be possible to look back over the data for the car and thus get a head start on anyone starting out with a brand new package. The disadvantages of buying second hand are often that cars for sale are either JMA cars that people have driven until they leave the sport or are JS cars whose driver has graduated to JM. This is not always a disadvantage, however if your plan was to drive the same chassis for an entire career then a steel JS car will not be able to be upgraded to a JMA. By the same token, a JMA will likely come equipped with a 7.90 second engine and so you will almost certainly have to put a JS engine in it and slow it down if you are buying for an entry level 8 year old. Though it is not inconceivable, it is not likely that a JMA car and team will have any data related to that car running as a JS and it is definitely not going to be the case that anyone selling a JS will be able to tell you anything meaningful about the cars potential in JM and JMA.

New cars are available from a couple of European chassis manufacturers and a far greater number of USA based specialists. It is worth remembering that these cars are a half scaled version of a full top fuel car. This does not mean that they are half as complex. In fact, as one reputable chassis builder once commented "there is almost as much work in a junior chassis as there is in a full size car, only in a junior everything is more difficult to do". What this indicates is that buyers should not expect a chassis to be cheap! New chassis from the US can cost as much as $8, 0000.00. This price will also attract import duty and shipping costs. One could commission a European builder to be able to construct the chassis for slightly less, yet all the peripherals such as wheels and tyres will almost exclusively be imported from the US as well, and therefore a European built rolling chassis is often not much cheaper than an American car.

The reasons for selecting one particular car may be linked to availability and budget; however there are other items to consider before committing to a particular car. Will your child be able to fit in the car for the expected duration of their career? Cars which have their pedals on a movable system like a ladder rack mean that the car can grow with the child. If the car can be fitted with a lay down seat, it will last a team much longer if the child becomes too tall.

In recent years there has been a profusion of cars with suspension. The benefit of a suspension car over a hard tail car is difficult to quantify, but if we think about the physics of the launch of a race car, it is clear to see what the thinking is. Working with Newton's first law it is clear that when sitting stationary at the start line, the car is at rest, and will remain so until a force acts upon it. This force will be the torque applied via the drive train to the rear wheels. Newton's second law states that the action of a force upon a body gives it acceleration in the direction of the force. Since the application of this force is not in the direction of travel; as the wheel is turning, therefore the vector of the force applied is not forwards in the direction of travel. The car will begin to accelerate in the opposite direction to the vector of the force applied. If we consider the shape of the wheel that is turning, we can see that the initial acceleration will not be straight ahead, but will actually be upwards and forwards. The equation for the force applied is F=ma where the force (F) = Mass (m) x Acceleration (a). The units used are kilograms and meters per second, where a force capable of accelerating one kilogram of mass at one meter per second in the direction of the applied force is referred to as one Newton so it can be seen that the 17th century physicist actually had quite a lot to say about dragsters!

A typical junior dragster and pilot (excluding any weight added to slow the car for class rules) will have a mass equivalent to roughly 100kg, and we want to accelerate the car to 35 meters per second (around 78MPH/125 KPH) within 8 seconds, then we need a force of 100 x (35/8) = 437 Newton's. However we are not going to be able to apply this force in the intended direction of travel, therefore we must expect the car to react by compressing its rear tyres and perhaps even lifting, or at least transferring its weight from the front to the rear. On a solid chassis car, there is nowhere for the chassis to flex enough to diminish these effects, therefore suspension cars were developed to allow the rear of the car to move independently of the rest of the chassis in an effort to translate more of the angular momentum into forward momentum. Whether this works or not is a point of discussion. The physics of the actions and reactions suggests that a significant portion of the force applied by the vehicle, whether solid chassis or suspension is "wasted" in lifting the front and squatting the rear, however this energy is stored in the compression of a spring in a suspension car and released as the spring extends. In practice this is exactly the same in a solid chassis car, but the energy is stored as compression in the tyres and the weight transfer from the front end. One could argue for hours over the relative merits of a suspension car against a solid chassis car, but at the end of the day we are dealing with junior dragsters which are unlikely to be producing much more than 50 hp, it seems the argument is practically meaningless. There may be a small advantage to a suspension car, but when considered as a whole it is more a question of budget, aesthetics and availability than it is a question of performance.

Tyres and tyre pressures

Junior Dragsters run on specialist tyres that are usually imported from the USA. Tyres do wear out eventually but the common thought that dragsters wear out tyres rapidly does not have much truth to it. Tyres harden over time but this hardening can be reduced by treating the rubber with either a proprietary tyre softener or more commonly by the application of a light spray of a product such as WD40 which is sprayed onto the tyre and then wiped off allowing the solvents in the product to soften the upper surface of the rubber and thus prolong the useful life. Tyres last for several seasons if managed well and if they avoid punctures.

Setting tyre pressures is important as a key means of speeding up or slowing down cars in both reaction times and on track ET times. A harder tyre (more air pressure) may spin off the line where a softer tyre (lower air pressure) can cause a car to "bog" or react slowly. Junior

Stock dragsters should be run with higher tyre pressures because the relatively low power of the stock engines means that tyre spin is not normally a problem and squatting or bogging on the line is less of an issue. Junior stock cars can effectively stick to the start line on a fully prepped track which can seriously impede reaction times, therefore minimising the contact patch by running high tyre pressures can help to reduce this impact. Higher powered cars in the JM and JMA classes need to maximise power delivery whilst maintaining wheel speed up the track so the tyre pressure must be optimised so that the car can leave the line without spinning the tyre but also without risking sticking to the line. A tyre pressure between 5 and 10 psi for Junior modified and modified advanced cars will produce a reasonable performance and test runs can provide a much smaller range of tyre pressures of perhaps one psi either side of an optimum pressure. Performance of cars and drivers varies from day to day and so it is possible to raise or lower the tyre pressure to compensate for track conditions. If the driver is reacting a little too fast and pulling red lights, we find we can speed up or slow down the reaction by simply adding or removing half a pound of pressure. Generally we find that lowering tyre pressures speeds up a reaction time whilst raising them speeds up an ET. This was the case for the authors particular set up and may vary from team to team. Experimentation is the key. On our home track we, as a team amassed hundreds of data points to clearly show that (for our particular set up) there was no practical benefit in running any tyre pressure below 6psi, in fact reaction times became unpredictable and ET's dropped away. Equally above 8psi the same occurred. We always ran a tyre pressure between 6 and 8psi and opted for a starting point for any event of either 7 or 7.5psi dependant on whether we thought the track was green. We would then go around for our first qualifying lap and see where the driver was on the tree and how the lap went. If he was a little late on the tree we would drop 0.25psi and if he was too quick we would add the same. This became a key part of our tuning strategy as we amassed more and more data. As a result of this we were usually able to qualify in the top five. On race day this was also invaluable as a tuning tool. Knowing we could raise or lower our tyre pressure accordingly to either slow down the reaction time to guard against red lights, or alternatively to raise or lower our dial in was a massive advantage. Due to the handicap start, a JMA car can be sitting on the line for a long time if it is competing against a JS entry; Some degree of control over how long the car has to wait can be gained by changing the tyre pressure to slow the predicted ET. This minimises the waiting time and also serves to reduce the driver stress which always helps.

Engines.

Junior dragster engines may initially seem to be a bewildering array of different manufacturers, types, codes and looks. Broadly speaking though, there are only a few types. These are principally either produced by, or based upon the design of, Briggs and Stratton single cylinder engines originally designed for lawn mowers, pumps and snow blowers. The junior stock engines are mostly Briggs and Stratton small displacement petrol engines, sometimes made specifically for junior racing, but also common across other applications. Junior Modified engines are larger displacement and often run on methanol, whilst Junior modified advanced engines are exclusively methanol and are almost always manufactured by a race engine builder but following the dimensions and patterns of a basic Briggs and Stratton design. Dependent upon age, these engines power the class from entry level to a racers final season. There is no rule in junior dragster that says a driver must move on a level, therefore it is possible for a driver to run a junior stock from the age of 8 – 18, although this is unlikely since the power output of a junior stock engine is likely to be too low to haul a teenager up the track in anything like a representative time. It is therefore common for JD's to have at least 2 engines throughout their life.

Whilst it is not uncommon for junior racers to be the children of hot rodders, drag racers and petrol heads, it is also not at all uncommon for parents with no mechanical knowledge to become involved in racing supporting their children. If you are fully conversant with internal combustion engines then please feel free to skip the next section, if however you are among those parents that find themselves bewildered by the workings of the engine and are therefore forced to send your engines away for all work to be completed by a third party, then perhaps this section might allow you to be more involved and to understand a little more of what is going on and how you can affect and influence the performance. This section is exclusively based upon Briggs and Stratton type single cylinder racing engines of the type's common in Junior Dragster racing. The principles described are common for all internal combustion engines, but the configurations, specifications and measurements will be different for other engines.

How the engine works

Internal combustion (IC) engines operate on either the two stroke or four stroke principle. Though it is not common for two stroke engines to be used in junior drag racing, it is worth explaining the principle differences between two and four stroke operation here.

Engines operating on the two stroke principle have a port (which may be controlled by a disc or reed valve) placed in the cylinder wall at a point slightly below the middle of the piston travel. With the piston at top dead centre (TDC) this port is covered by the piston and is therefore closed. The action of the piston travelling to its TDC point creates a low pressure zone in the crank case which sucks air through the carburettor, mixing with fuel in the process. The fuel air charge is sucked into the crank case. As the piston travels back downwards towards its Bottom Dead Centre (BDC) position it creates a high pressure zone below it which forces the air and fuel out of the crank case and up the inlet tract which is uncovered by the piston and is now open. The low pressure in the cylinder caused by the movement of the piston is the reverse of the high pressure in the crank case and so the fuel/air charge flows into the cylinder. As the piston moves back towards TDC it covers the inlet port again and so seals the fuel/air mixture into the combustion chamber and compresses it before it is ignited around the TDC point and the piston is forced back down. An exhaust port is placed in the piston wall opposite the inlet port and this is also uncovered as the piston travels downwards. The hot exhaust gasses exit the piston through this exhaust port and are vented to the atmosphere.

Engines operating on the four stroke principle complete two strokes of the piston per revolution of the crank. If the engine is thought of as commencing operation at tdc, then the downward stroke is the first of the four. This is the induction stroke in which the intake valve is open and the engine can suck air through the carburettor, mixing the air with the fuel in the process. At or around bdc the intake valve closes and the piston begins to travel back up the cylinder. The air and fuel mixture is sealed into the cylinder by the head gasket, head and piston rings. This is the compression stroke and is accompanied just before tdc by the spark which ignites the fuel air mixture just as the piston goes over tdc. The ignition of the compressed air and fuel causes an explosion and a rapid expansion of gases just above the piston causing it to travel back down the cylinder rapidly. This downward stroke is where the engine makes all its power and hence this is called the power stroke. At or around bdc the exhaust valve begins to open and the piston travels back to tdc pushing the burnt gases out into the tailpipe in the exhaust stroke. As the piston reaches tdc, the cycle is ready to start again.

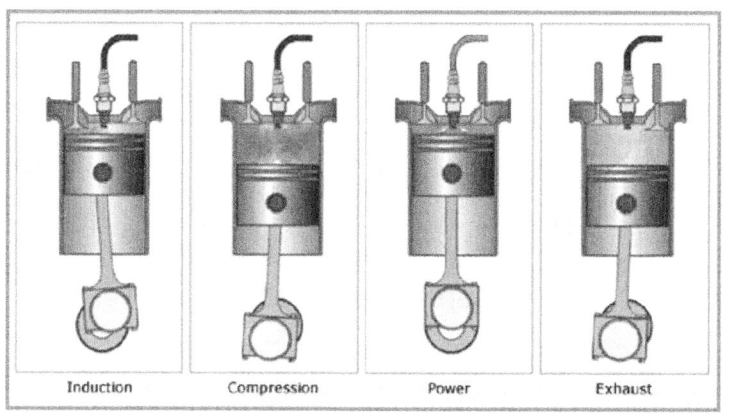

| Induction | Compression | Power | Exhaust |

This process is the same for all four stroke engines regardless of the number of pistons or the engine displacement. Each piston in a V8 or V12 works in exactly this manner, the only difference being that a multi cylinder engine has a piston on the power stroke turning the crank and aiding another piston on its compression stroke. Single cylinder engines do not have this added force and so they must store some energy in the flywheel. Flywheels are a rotating mass attached to the crank with the purpose of storing energy. If you imagine spinning a bicycle wheel by hand and then grabbing it to stop it spinning, you can imagine the principle of a flywheel, the work you did to get the wheel spinning in the first instance needs to be almost matched by the force needed to stop the spin, the wheel has "stored" the energy taken to make it spin and will continue to spin until something else makes it stop. This is how the flywheel on a junior dragster works. The power stroke makes the flywheel spin fast and the energy is partially stored in the flywheel and recovered to push the piston back up the cylinder for the exhaust, induction and compression strokes. On a Junior Dragster the flywheel has two purposes, firstly it stores the rotational energy of the engine as described, and secondly it carries the magnets which cause the field effect in the coil and generate the spark.

Junior dragster engines explained

Junior dragster engines are almost exclusively internal combustion (IC) engines. We are starting to see some electric power units coming into racing but at the time of writing they are expensive and quite rare. All the IC engines in the class operate on the four stroke principle. That is to say that each piston travels the length of its stroke four times for each occasion it makes power. There are four common measurements discussed for a piston engine, these are the bore, which is the diameter of the cylinder; the stroke, which is the distance that the piston travels from its highest position to its lowest position; the displacement, which is the cubic capacity of the cylinder and the compression ratio which is the relationship between the volume of the cylinder when the piston is at its lowest position and the volume remaining when the piston has travelled through its full stroke to its highest position.

The highest position is referred to as "Top dead centre" usually shortened to tdc. The lowest position is referred to as "bottom dead centre" usually shortened to bdc. The piston operates inside the cylinder and is therefore marginally smaller than the bore. It is sealed against the walls of the cylinder by a number of piston rings which fit into grooves machined into the piston wall.

Piston rings

The piston rings have three main purposes:

1. To seal the combustion chamber
2. To transfer heat from the piston to the cylinder walls
3. To control the flow of oil

The number of rings varies between engine and piston design and applications however there will always be at least one compression ring and one oil control ring. Compression rings are usually a solid construction whilst oil control rings are generally a composite of thinner rings sandwiching a corrugated ring. Regardless of the number of rings, the compression rings always fit into the top groove(s) whilst the oil control rings fit into the bottom one(s). Unless gapless rings are used, rings are invariably supplied too large and require "gapping" to ensure a good fit. Advice and folklore about correct ring gaps varies but a reasonable ring gap is in the region of 0.004" (0.1mm) per inch (25.4mm) of cylinder bore. Ring gaps should be arranged so that they are out of line on the piston wall, i.e. the gap in the top ring does not line up with the gap in the ring directly below it. The pistons that I use in my engines have one compression ring and one oil control ring (made up of two plane rings and one corrugated ring) therefore I have four ring gaps. When constructing my engines I favour positioning one gap every ninety degrees of piston.

Connecting Rod

The connecting rod is the length of metal that joins the piston to the crank. Connecting rods are usually delivered in at least two parts (although often manufactured as one piece units which are subsequently cut), the main rod has the small end (the end that connects to the piston) which is fully cast and contains the bearing for the wrist pin (gudgeon pin) which joins the rod to the piston. The rod itself is a solid item encompassing half of the big end journal, which is the circular section that fits on to the crank. The other half of the big end journal is made up of the end cap through which the big end bolts will pass to secure the end cap to the main rod clamping the crank between them. This also will contain the big end bearings. These are plain bearings which are smooth pieces of metal formed to the shape of the big end journal and designed to provide a replaceable layer between the rod and the crank so that the crank does not wear the rod away. The big end bearings also contain oil holes and grooves to allow oil to form a protective film between the crank and the rod bearings. Rod lengths vary according to the desired end stroke so care must be taken to ensure that any rod you are purchasing is the right length for the engine you are fitting it to. Too short and the engine will not make as much power, too long and the piston will hit the cylinder head before tdc and the engine will not function.   The ideal rod length allows the piston to reach tdc with its top surface flush with the top rim of the cylinder. The bottom of the connecting rod

Piston

The piston is mounted onto the top of the connecting rod by a wrist pin (gudgeon pin) which passes through holes on the piston skirt and through the top of the connecting rod. The wrist pin is held in place by clips which locate into grooves machined in the piston skirt to hold the ends of the wrist pin snugly and evenly spaced in the piston. There are two types of retainers which are common in these engines. The simple circlip which resembles a horseshoe with two flat tangs with holes in at the ends. Circlip pliers car be used to remove these retainers easily and quickly. The second type is the spiralok which are flat spiral retainers which need to be fed into the groove patiently and with a great deal of care. These clips are reportedly better at retaining wrist pins as they are less likely to break or pop out of the groove, but they are extremely fiddly to set and difficult to remove.

Cylinder Head

The cylinder head is a separate element in the engine which is held on to the main block by a number of head bolts. It is separated from the main block by a gasket which is constructed from a softer material (often copper in junior engines). This gasket is there to seal the joint between cylinder head and block. Both of these elements are constructed from hard materials as they need to handle the temperatures and pressures generated by the engine. The softer material of the gasket is compressed between the two, often with some gasket sealant as additional help, and allows the head to form a gas tight seal with the block. The cylinder head will be machined on its inside with recesses to allow the valves to operate. It will also contain the combustion chamber and have a threaded hole to allow a spark plug to be fitted protruding into the combustion chamber to ignite the fuel air mixture.

Flywheels and coils

The flywheel magnets and the coil in a junior dragster work together to generate sufficient electrical current to jump the gap between the electrodes of a spark plug, creating a spark to ignite fuel in the combustion chamber. As already discussed, the engine has a flywheel, to which a permanent magnet is attached. Each time the flywheel revolves, the magnet passes the coil which, as its name suggests is a long coil of copper wire. As discovered by Faraday in the 1830's, a magnet passing a coil of wire will generate an electrical current within the coil of wire. This current isn't strong enough to jump the gap across the spark plug electrodes, however, but Faraday also discovered that current generated within a coil produces its own magnetic field which can then be used to generate current in a second coil. According Faraday's law, the voltage produced in a coil is proportional to the amount of turns within the coil itself. In the most commonly used junior dragster coils, the primary coil is comprised of around 75 turns, whilst the secondary coil has more than 4,000 turns. This means that the permanent magnet generates a current and associated magnetic field within the primary coil which then goes on to develop a current of about 10,000 amps, which is sufficient to jump the gap between the spark plug electrodes. The spark ignites the fuel, and the engine starts making the flywheel spin thus making the magnet pass the coil again and keeping the process going.

Carburettors

Fuel is supplied to the engine through a carburettor which is a device to mix the right amount of fuel and the right amount of air for the engine to run efficiently as possible. If the mix has too much fuel in it, the engine cannot burn the fuel in the time available and also cannot get rid of the volume of fumes and so will tend to run but run very badly, while too little fuel will make the engine run too hot and also not produce enough power per stroke to continue running. Getting the right amount of fuel and air into the piston to be burned efficiently is the job of the carburetor.

A carburettor is basically a tube with an adjustable plate across it called the throttle plate. The throttle plate controls how much air can flow through the carb, the wider the throttle is opened, the less restriction (throttling) there is of the air flow and so the more air can flow through to the piston. Inside the carb there is a narrowing called a venturi. As air flows through this narrow point it speeds up creating a lower pressure in the jets which are openings from the fuel bowl at the base of the carb. This causes fuel to be drawn up into the air flow and transported into the piston. These components form the basis of any carb. In simple terms, the driver presses the throttle pedal which is connected to the throttle plate and causes the throttle plate to open; allowing more air to flow through the carb which creates a bigger venturi vacuum that ultimately sends more fuel into the engine, creating more power. In order to ensure that there is always sufficient fuel in the bowl of the carburettor to be entrained into the air flow, a float is positioned in the base of the carburettor which forms the float bowl. When there is sufficient fuel in the float bowl the floats rise and cause the fuel valve to block the fuel inlet stopping any more fuel arriving, as the fuel is used the floats follow the fuel level and open the fuel valve.

The throttle plate has a small area cut away so that even when the throttle plate is fully closed some air can still flow to the piston. This air flow is not generally sufficient to entrain any fuel through the main jet and so a secondary small jet is also built in to the carb called the idle jet which allows sufficient fuel to be entrained in the low air flow to the cylinder to keep the engine running.

Fuel pumps

Fuel is supplied to the carburettor from the fuel tank via a small pump which operates by using the increases and decreases in pressure in the intake manifold to move a diaphragm. The other side of the diaphragm is connected to the fuel lines via two non-return valves. When the Intake valve is open, air and fuel rush through the manifold and draw in some air from the dry side of the diaphragm causing it to move outwards. The resultant vacuum on the wet side of the diaphragm sucks fuel through the first non-return valve from the tank into the pump body. When the intake valve closes, a spring pushes the diaphragm back to its normal position and pushes the fuel out through the second non return valve into the carburettor float bowl.

Clutches

Any engine driving any application, whether it is a dragster or a snow mobile needs some method of stopping the drive. In simple applications such as a leaf blower or generator, the method of stopping the drive may be simply to switch off the engine. In more complex applications such as cars, dragsters, motorcycles etc. there must be a device installed in the drive train that de-couples the engine drive from the final drive so that the vehicle can be stationary with the engine running. In higher applications this may also be part of the gearing mechanism where to remain stationary the gearbox may be put into a neutral gear allowing the engine to spin but not providing drive.

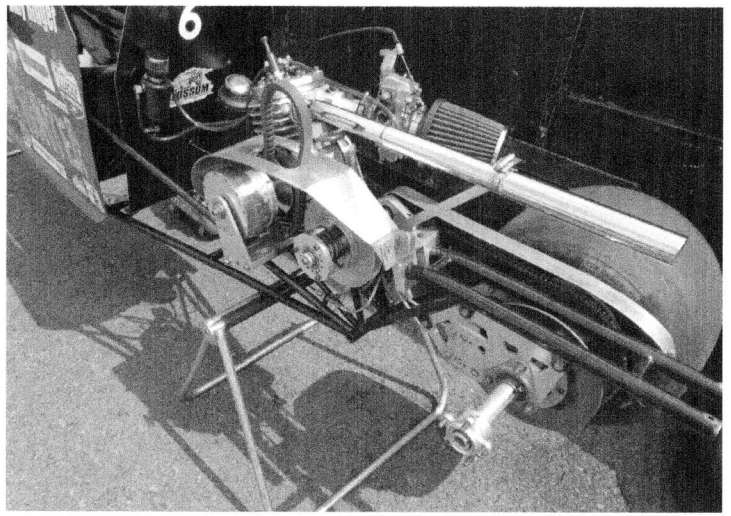

Junior dragsters are not allowed gears under the current rules, and as is common across all drag racing, are required to remain stationary on the line before the tree runs and the race commences. To achieve this Junior Dragsters are fitted with a clutch which also doubles as the gearbox of the dragster. Two types of clutch dominate the class, namely the Polar and the

Shockwave clutch designs. Both clutch designs work on similar principles. As engine revs increase a weighted roller is bought into contact with an angle block which causes the two outer sheaves (plates) of the clutch to come together, clamping the drive belt and raising the primary gear ratio. At the same time, the belt, which is of fixed length, is drawn downwards between the sheaves of the driven clutch unit which has the effect of lowering the driven ratio.

At start up and engine idle the primary clutch sheaves allow the belt to run on the main shaft. The belt is held at the top rim of the Driven sheaves

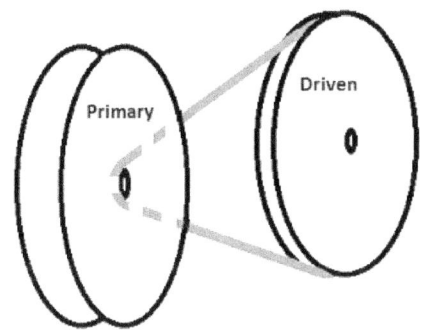

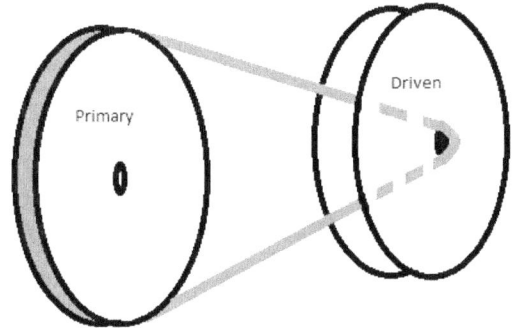

When engine revs rise and the clutch weights "fly" the belt is drawn up the primary sheaves and down the driven sheaves providing a higher drive ratio.

Opinion is divided between racers and parents over which is the best clutch for the class. Users of both clutch systems are fiercely brand loyal. Polar clutches are an older design and require regular maintenance and cleaning to continue in smooth operation. Shockwave clutches require less maintenance which is reportedly easier but they have a slightly higher initial cost. It is certain that cars equipped with either brand have won and continue to win races. Newer designs from both manufacturers have addressed brand specific issues and now it would be fair to say that the main difference is loyalty and personal choice. The author has always used Polar clutches, but has worked on Shockwave equipped cars. In cases where teams exhibit good maintenance regimes and check their equipment regularly no material difference has been noted. A poorly maintained car and clutch will inevitably suffer some failure either through the clutch or any other poorly maintained item.

Slowing cars down.

Because of the existence of the class index, it may be necessary to slow a car down to stay within the rules. This may sound counter intuitive but we must remember that the class index is there for the safety of all competitors and officials and therefore it must be obeyed. Engines can be the most expensive part of the whole set up and so it is common for teams to run an engine which will see them through in more than one class, i.e. JM and JMA. This means that it is common for engines capable of running in the high 7 second region to be powering dragsters with drivers who are restricted to the 8.9 second bracket. There are several ways to achieve this, some of which are more consistent and successful than others.

Ballast

Adding ballast to a car increases the weight and therefore effectively reduces the power to weight ratio and slows the car down. The general rule of thumb is that each 1lb of weight slows a car down by 1/100th of a second; therefore 10lb will take 1/10th of a second off the ET. There are specific ways in which ballast can be attached to the car, and restrictions and limitations to where it can be. It is common for cars to carry weight tanks beneath and/or slightly behind the driver. This position, in front of the engine and behind the driver is the most effective position for weight to be applied. The tank is usually a metal box with a screw cap or latched lid, this is generally filled with lead shot as the most common ballast. Weight tanks may also be fitted behind the rear wheels or in the front of the car under the bodywork and in front of the driver's feet. Weight placed behind the wheels is less effective since it actually increases traction and therefore the slowing effect is partially counteracted by a secondary effect of speeding the car up. Weight placed behind the wheels is therefore less effective and may require up to 15lb per 10th rather than the generally accepted 10lb. Weight placed in front of the driver is also marginally less effective but is still a better compromise than placing it behind the rear wheels.

Weight must not be "adjustable" from the driving position, and therefore must always be placed out of the drivers reach. It must be secure and attached to the car by bolts or clamps with a secure fastener. Weight may not be taped or cable tied into position. Refer to your rule book for a full description of the rules for your specific class and association.

Air restrictors

Cars may also be slowed down by restricting the airflow through the carburettor. This can be achieved by making up a simple plate in 0.5mm sheet. The plate should be sized to allow it to be bolted between the intake manifold and the cylinder block. Using a conical hole cutter the plate should be cut out to a diameter smaller than the rated carburettor diameter, e.g. 28mm for a 33mm Mikuni carburettor. This will have the effect of throttling the airflow such that the engine cannot flow the full volume of air it is capable of, and therefore a lower amount of fuel air mixture will enter the piston and the car will run slower. When using this method it is useful to make a number of these restrictors in stepped sizes starting at 70% of the carburettor diameter and ending at 95% of diameter. It is unlikely that the effect of anything larger than 95% will be measurable and anything smaller than 70% means you have the wrong carburettor and engine combination.

This method of slowing cars is by far the most consistent.

Throttle stops

It is possible to restrict the travel of the throttle pedal through use of a throttle stop. This could be a bolt, threaded or passed through the throttle pedal which makes contact with a solid plate or block at the required point of throttle travel. On Junior stock cars and to some extent junior modified cars, this method can be effective. The throttle stop can be adjusted by screwing in or unscrewing the bolt through the pedal thereby allowing more or less throttle travel before the bolt makes contact with the stop and effectively locks out any further travel to control the ET or speed. This method is not 100% effective on the larger JMA cars since the most common carburettor used in this class is capable of flowing enough air and fuel at even half throttle to allow the engine to see almost full power. For this reason, there is little or no point in fine adjustment of the throttle slide. One can play around with altering the throttle slide position on these engines by fractions of inches and it will have such a tiny effect as to be negligible. However on lower powered cars, especially small displacement petrol cars (as in Junior Stock) this can be effective.

Timing

If the car needs to be slowed down by only a small amount (less than a tenth of a second for example), this may be achieved by altering the timing on the flywheel. Most JD engines have a movable coil mounting which can be moved to either left or right to advance or retard the timing. Moving the coil to the right has the effect of making the spark happen later so it is igniting the fuel after TDC when the piston was already on its way back down and the compression is reducing. This means that the force of the explosion is reduced and the power delivered is equally reduced. This method can also be used to fine tune engine performance.

Gearing

Junior dragster final drive is delivered by a gear and chain arrangement attached to the secondary clutch shaft (called the jackshaft). There are numerous sizes and tooth patterns available for both the small front sprocket and the larger rear gear. Gearing ratios are a useful way to slow or accelerate a car, however some understanding of the trade off between speed and torque needs to be considered. The optimum ratios are very different for the different classes, A junior stock engine does not produce a great deal of torque and therefore needs a different ratio to a JMA high power high torque engine. However, as an exercise and to demonstrate how gearing can slow a car, we can see that: The rear tyre is approximately 56" in circumference, and we know that the finish line is 660' away, we also can work out that (without wheel spin) the engine will need to turn the wheels 142 times to get us over the finish line. At a 7.5:1 ratio, that requires approximately 1060 full rotations of the front sprocket. If we imagine that the front sprocket we are using has 12 teeth, our rear sprocket must have 90. If we raise this to 91 or 92 teeth we achieve a ratio of 7.6:1 which will now take 1074 revolutions of the front to carry us the same distance. If our effective engine speed remains the same, we can see that this will slow us down. This theory can similarly be used to speed a car up, although it is not the simple case that fewer teeth on the rear equates to a quicker car. Other considerations related to the amount of torque produced by the motor, the clutch ratios and the belt condition come into play but having the ability to slow a car or speed it up through a selection of front and rear sprockets is useful.

Data Recorders

Many cars in competition today are fitted with data recorders. These units are capable of recording the engine rpm, cylinder and exhaust gas temperatures and jack shaft rpm. It is possible to analyse the data from each run in the form of numerical or graphic formats and to make tuning decisions based upon the data gathered from the car. In practical terms however there are other variables which influence performance outside these data such as air temperature, wind speed, track temperature, fuel temperature etc. Many teams use the data recorder simply as a rev counter display to set start line revs and seldom if ever download and analyse the remaining data from the unit. I have always found this to be somewhat questionable as a startline technique. Certainly teams who use this technique always start at a similar amount of rpm's but they do not have any grasp of what power those rpm's were producing. Climatic conditions vary and therefore so does the amount of power produced per stroke of the engine. Anyone who has ever seen a dyno curve will understand that power and torque are measured across the rev range and the air temperature, moisture content and air pressure are always stated in the graph. On a hot dry day an engine has a very different characteristic that it would have on a cool humid day. Data recorders do not tell a team any of that data on the startline, though certain models can record this data for the day. We never ran with a data recorder and we had as much and in many cases more success than other teams that did. Data recorders would perhaps be useful to teams in a position to interpret and react to the data they provide, however in most cases teams do not use it. In this respect data recorders would seem to be an expensive add on to cars that is simply not required. If the team are interested however there is a great deal that can be achieved through using the outputs of a recorder. High cylinder head temperatures may be indicative of lean running conditions whilst mismatches between engine and jack shaft speeds indicate clutch slip or wheel spin. Engine and jack shaft speeds are also indicative of clutch set up and can be used to tune clutch bob weights and spring tensions as well as indicating belt wear. All of these conditions can be readily addressed leading to improved running and better consistency. As a crew chief, the author has never used a data recorder, preferring a home built excel based spreadsheet which captures all known variables.

Qualification and competition.

Junior dragsters qualify for competition by the driver's reaction time to the tree. It is common for the top five or more qualification times to be below one hundredth of a second and often the number one qualifier will have a reaction time below one thousandth of a second. It is not possible for a human to react to a signal in this amount of time. Additionally it is not possible for a simple machine without any electronic aids to react to a human input in such a time. If we analyse the process then it is possible to understand how these drivers are achieving these feats.

In the first instance we must understand how quickly the driver can react. Studies indicate that the average human reaction time is in the order of 0.25 seconds, so if drivers were reacting to the green light, this would be the time in which the majority of the junior dragster reactions would sit. However we then need to factor in some other elements. If a driver pressed their accelerator pedal as the green light came on, the throttle plate in the carburettor would open and the engine would start to make power. It then needs to engage the drive belt and start to move through the 14 inches of distance until the stage beam is remade and the reaction time is logged. This process takes an additional 0.1 – 0.3 seconds, so a well set up car with an above average driver would still only register a reaction time of between 0.3 and 0.5 seconds.

How then can we explain that drivers are regularly recording reaction times which are in the order of 0.001 seconds?

The answer is that drivers learn to anticipate the green light. Each driver builds up their own methods and understanding of their car and picks a point on the tree at which they can press the pedal and pull away without the stage beam reconnecting and turning on the red light. In practice there are many methods which a driver can adopt. Some have a rhythm which they begin to count out when they see the first amber; others simply experiment on the tree and work out where they need to go to achieve a quick time. Since the timing between the bulbs is known and standard across all race tracks, we know that there is 0.5 seconds between the third amber and the green. Therefore if you have a car and driver package that can take the whole of that 0.5 seconds to react and get moving, then it is clear to see that pressing the accelerator as the third amber lights will mean the car leaves the line round about the point that the green comes on. This means that the driver has half a second from first to second amber and then half a second until the third one lights, so if they count or beat out those times, they should put the pedal to the floor exactly as the third amber comes on. Drivers have used mantra's such as tick, tick TOCK where they hit the pedal on the third word. Working out your best strategy is a personal issue, but working it out well can mean the difference between number one qualifier and last place consistently.

It may seem that the reaction time is entirely down to the driver; however the crew chief can influence things as well. Crew chiefs set start line revs which can be decreased slightly to slow down a reaction time or increased to speed it up. If the driver is constantly hitting red lights or 0.1 reaction times the crew chief may choose to raise or lower tyre pressures or alter start revs to compensate. It is the role of the crew chief to manage the car so the driver can hit the reaction times required for higher qualifying positions. We have seen many drivers who can hit 0.05 second reactions almost every time, but that struggle to achieve lower numbers. These drivers are obviously following a set routine and it is working for them, but their crew chief has not realised that they can help by letting the driver always do the same thing but subtly modifying the way the car reacts so that the car comes to the driver rather than vice versa. It is well worth experimenting with tyre pressures and engine revs to see if you can help your driver. If you do this though, remember to log what you did and what the effect was, thus allowing you to re-create the conditions that work best every time.

Once qualifications are complete, competition and eliminations commence. Dependent upon the number of cars entered in the race, the ladder will be created such that one half of the qualifying order will race the other half in a knock out competition. The usual format for a 16 car ladder means that number one qualifier would race the number 9, 2 would race 10 etc. However the ladders are created so that the number one and number two qualifiers would not meet each other until the final if indeed they won all their intervening races.

Winning a competition round is fundamentally achieved by being the first car to cross the finish line without breaking out. This is not always the case, and we shall see some of the other ways in which a race can be won in more detail later. Firstly though we will concentrate on the primary method of winning. Breaking out is the term given to a race in which a driver crosses the finish line in less time than they had entered as their dial in. The dial in time of a car is set by the team prior to the race commencing. Dial in times can be displayed on the car or on a board carried by a team member. The selected dial in will be displayed on the timing board above the drivers lane. It is important to ensure as crew that you look at the timing boards and make sure that the time displayed is the time you wanted. Failure to do so will mean that your driver will be judged against the wrong time and that the handicap delay will also be incorrect. The dial in can be adjusted right up until the car is about to enter pre-stage, but if your car has a dial in board attached to it, it is also important to remember that touching any part of the car once it has crossed the blue line a little way before the pre stage beams is an infringement for which your driver will be disqualified.

Setting dial in times.

Races are won and lost by tiny margins in most cases. Dial ins are a vital part of winning. When one first begins racing, setting the dial in may seem like a black art, but with time and experience, the process becomes easier and the dial in times become more accurate. Wind, track condition, air temperature and humidity play important roles in the performance of the car, but wind is probably the most influential of these. Junior dragsters are deeply affected by head and tail winds and may be susceptible to crosswinds in some cases. Learning how your car reacts to wind conditions will help immensely in narrowing your dial in's accordingly. In the first instance one can use the quickest time that the car has run over the course of the race meeting so far. After this the time can be adjusted up or down dependent upon what has changed. A log of data is useful at this point. Many teams run with data loggers on the cars. These are devices which monitor cylinder head and exhaust gas temperatures, rpm's of both the engine and the jack shaft and potentially time and air temperature. I have yet to meet anyone racing in Europe that utilises the data fully, and I have never used a data logger on any of my cars. I do use an excel spreadsheet into which I log the time of the lap, dial in, RT, ET's from the timing ticket, speeds from the timing ticket and a commentary section in which we detail tyre pressures, weather conditions and anything of interest. This log also allows me to keep a running tally of laps completed which is useful for pin pointing oil changes, rod and piston changes etc. The accumulated data allows me to hone in on dial times by comparing equivalent times of day, temperatures, track conditions and wind speeds and directions. Using this we have managed to create a system which gives us a "window" of dial in times for the conditions and we can start to hone these over the course of the event. I have learned over the years to dial every race, whether it is in qualifications or eliminations.

Dial in's don't matter in qualification, but they do provide you with practice opportunities on the track that you will race in eliminations. Quite often the eliminations will commence on a different day than qualifications, so it is common to not get a practice lap on eliminations day. This provides an amount of worry to many teams, yet if they were constantly dialling their car for every run off the trailer, the uncertainty of a race day dial would be certainly diminished.

Winning races

In principle a race is won by the driver that crosses the line first without breaking out. There are however other ways in which the race result can be decided. A driver may red light which grants the win to the opponent. Both cars may break out in which case the win is awarded to the car that broke out by the least margin. Any car that touches the wall or crosses the centre line is immediately disqualified. This can prove interesting where a red light infringement had already happened in the other lane. Racing rules work on a first or worst principle, driving outside ones marked lane (either touching the wall or crossing the centre) is deemed as a worse infringement than a red light, so it is possible to red light and yet still win the race. A technical infringement can also result in a disqualification. This is caused when any team member other than the driver has contact with the car once any part of it has crossed a line which is painted on the track a short distance ahead of the pre stage line. Any car receiving a technical or blue line infringement is automatically disqualified. Cars can also lose races by breaking class indexes (11.90 seconds for JS, 8.9 seconds for JM and 7.9 seconds for JMA). Should the driver break the class index by 2/10ths or less, they will be given a warning, and asked to slow the car down. A second infringement under 2/10ths may result in exclusion from the event at the race steward's discretion. Breaking class index by more than 4/10 second can and frequently does result in removal from the event.

It can readily be seen that there are many more ways to lose a race than there are to win! No matter what the racetrack bores tell you, there is only one sure fire way of winning a race. Get a good reaction time and hit your dial in. It is not possible to beat a car that leaves the line with a perfect reaction time and hits its dial in perfectly. We once raced against a competitor who went 0.00024 on the tree and ran 8.9901 on an 8.99 dial. No matter how good we thought we were that day, we could only have won that race by being one or two ten thousandths of a second away from either breaking out or red lighting. That kind of package is pretty much unbeatable. Therefore this is what you must try to achieve. Practice trees and race seat time will allow you to improve your reaction times. Understanding your car through accumulated data will allow you to hone in on dial in. The simple answer to how you win races is practice, concentration, hard work and devotion. It is not uncommon for rumours to circulate that car x is "cheating". Before you get involved in the conspiracy theories surrounding such accusations, consider the following; what would you need to do to a car to make it run perfectly? Firstly, it would need to be staged perfectly to the millimetre every time, so that a computer could take over the lights. Next it would have to run an exact straight line to the finish. Then there would have to be no variables such as track grip, wind, heat, air pressure etc. The computing power to do this patently exists, but the sensor pack required to run it would be highly noticeable.

Remember the adage – two cars start, one car loses, try not to be that one. When you are that one, work out why and don't do that again!

Dial the car every lap, and be honest with yourself. 20:20 hindsight is no use when you lost. Data is the only thing that will help you. If you think the conditions are right for the car to run a time, then log it. Compare what you logged to the time slip. Work out how close you were and keep doing it until your dial in predictions are accurate.

Holding numbers, sand bagging, running ahead and all the other terms you will hear are all methods other teams will try and use to beat you.

There is no rule about dial ins except they must not be quicker than class index. Some teams, especially those with a big chase down, e.g. a JMA against a stock car, may choose to dial slower than they think the car is going to go. This allows them to not be in stage for as long, and also for the driver to run up the track and catch the opponent a good distance before the finish line. Well trained and practiced drivers can then brake and come in over dial but still ahead of the opposition. However, as I said at the beginning of this section, if the opposition had a good RT and is close on dial, this still won't work. Some teams choose to run slow in qualification so the opposition are surprised when the race day dial is a lot quicker than they thought. Others go the other way around.

Dialling a car marginally quicker than it is capable of is the most common strategy. This gives you a safety window, but if the opponent was on their game, they are still unbeatable.

It is worth reiterating. Drag racing is the simplest of sports made complicated by the people who do it. Get a good RT, run close to or on dial and you are pretty much unbeatable. Practice, rehearse, visualise, and put all the elements together and you will be consistent and feared.

When you are fortunate enough to win a race the timing ticket you receive will detail the winner and also provide a win margin. This is the amount of time by which you won the race. It is very common for win margins to be in the order of thousandths of a second where two drivers were close on their dials. Most of these races are won on the tree. Right at the beginning of this book I said that a perfect light with a perfect dial in was unbeatable. Hopefully we can see that this is true in so far as the lap is completed without a technical rule infringement. Drivers and teams that learn to deliver good reaction times and who have honed in on their dial times and understood the relationship between changing conditions and performance to dial in will always be a force to be reckoned with. It has been my experience that teams who rely on questionable tactics, start line and track games and other psychological tricks and stunts are the teams that do not understand the variables and therefore have to resort to other tactics. You could also take such behaviour as a compliment, since the people who engage in it must be so unsure of their ability to win against you in fair means have resorted to "tactics" to try and beat you. Stay honest, stay true to the ethos of the sport and be technically excellent and you will be able to look back on each and every win with equal pride. No-one likes losing, but a hollow victory is not even half as good as a solid clean win.

The games people play

At the beginning of this book I said "There is a lot of talk about tactics and methods, gamesmanship and strategy. As a beginner, the most important thing to remember is that the only person that you really have to race is yourself." This is the area in which this is most true. In your racing career you will hear lots of people discussing incredibly complex ways that they believe they can win. In reality, all the methods that people talk about are more often ways to lose a race than ways to win. The simple fact is that a perfect reaction time and a perfect ET will win every race. This combination cannot be beaten by any smart tactics, driving techniques or start line games. Therefore if one simply concentrates on setting an accurate dial-in and cutting good lights, you are half way to unbeatable. There really is no need for any other tactics, and actually it makes more sense for a driver to pull through a lap at full throttle all the way. It provides the team with data about the performance, speed, ET and the relationship these have to external factors including temperature, wind, air quality and density etc. All of this data will be invaluable when it comes to setting dial in's and progressing through rounds of competition.

Of course there are tactics and considerations that are worth remembering and that can be useful in one's race armoury. If a driver is aware of their dial in and also aware of the other car, they can take a view on where they are on track compared to the opponent. As already stated, races are won by the car that crosses the finish line first without breaking out. Also, as already discussed, running to a perfect dial in is unbeatable. Other factors do come into consideration, what if the wind that has been blowing all day and throughout qualifications has suddenly increased or decreased? What if the air density has changed? These and many more factors can increase or decrease a cars speed and affect its ET, so a driver does need to be aware of their position relative to the other car. At the JS level, it is probably best for a driver to just run flat out, with such a small amount of power available there is little they can do to change the outcome of a race. JM and JMA drivers however have more options. A smart driver who has cut a good light can look across the track at the opposite lane and see if the opposing car is close. In many cases, if the other car is not there one of three things has happened. Either the other driver has pulled a really bad light, or they have broken on the line or one of the two cars is off their dial by a margin. It is impossible for a driver to know if it is the other car that is running too slow, or they that are running too fast. In either case the wise driver may take their foot off the accelerator and coast through the line. If this is done towards the end of the lap it will shed only a tenth or two from the ET, but could be the difference between a breakout and win. Drivers with very powerful motors may be able to accelerate a little more if required, but most cars will be flat out at least by mid track, so if the you are not catching the car in front, either one of the cars is off its dial in, or you have a problem or pulled a terrible light. In this case there is little that can be done except drive through the line. If the opposing car has a significant lead over you, it is also not unusual to see them lift or brake as described above since they also will not know if it is they that are running too quick.

The rest of the tactics and methods employed by racers are broadly gamesmanship and I will here discuss just a few. I do not encourage or support such games, and the choice of a crew chief and driver that have the games played against them is simple, you either go along with it, or you take charge of the situation and manage it to your own advantage. One can actually take it as a compliment when a team decide that they want to play start line games with you. It basically means that they do not have enough confidence in their own ability to win and have to resort to other methods to try and unsettle you. The classic start line games are to take forever to come to the line or to stage, or to go into stage really quickly. Both are meant to fluster and unsettle the opposing driver. The ways to deal with these are as follows.

If an opponent decides to make you wait while they play around with things on their car, they are doing it to get your engine hot and possibly to make you start doubting whether you have enough fuel. Junior dragsters are often only fuelled for one race with very little spare fuel on board, fuel is weight and weight slows you down, therefore the least weight you carry, the quicker you will be. I have seen teams try and run an opponent's fuel down so that they will be running on fumes by the end of the lap. It didn't work and in playing this game, the protagonist managed to unsettle themselves so much they red lit, so it was fundamentally a pointless exercise. If you should find yourself in this position, and you believe that the opponent is trying to deliberately disadvantage you, there are options open to you. The teams that play these games are usually renowned for such behaviour, so in the first instance, when facing any such team, the prime option is to give them time, waiting until they are ready before you dial up your start line revs and approach the stage beams. This means that you have remained in charge of the situation and removed the problem. In some cases this will not be possible, and at these times it is important to stay calm, this is obviously not the effect that your opponent wants so you have once again retained control. If they continue to mess around, you should calmly bring your car into pre stage. Further messing around by the opponent will be dealt with by the start marshal, which has now put the pressure on to the opponent. Do not go beyond pre stage though. Courtesy must always prevail. Once you have lit the pre stage bulbs, allow the other car to come in to pre stage and then calmly creep forwards in to stage. The other car now only has seven seconds to come in to stage and start the race or they will be disqualified. In this way, you have retained control throughout the whole process and removed the advantage from the opponent. It is important to always remember that there may be a genuine reason why the opponent seems to be messing around, and you should always give them the benefit of the doubt, but still remain in charge of the situation. After all, they came to race, the same as you did, so remaining calm and keeping control is the best way for you to not only race, but race and win.

The other commonly employed method of unsettling opponents is for a car to drive straight in to stage before you have had a chance to even pre stage. Teams employ this tactic to try and rush you through your start line procedure and to either get a car disqualified under the seven second rule or to make a mistake and deep stage or red light. If an opponent does this to you, then the response is simple. Do not be rushed, remain calm and stay in control of the situation. The rules of staging, both written and unwritten say that when both cars are ready to approach the line, and the start marshal has instructed them to do so, they should approach the line and move in to pre stage. The car that goes in to pre stage first will stop and wait for the other car to come in, then once both pre stage lights for both lanes are lit, the car that went in first will go in to stage and the other one will follow within seven seconds. If a car goes in to full stage before you have approached the line, you should stop and wait for an instruction from the chief starter. If in the starter's opinion the other car has deliberately gone in to full stage to unsettle their opponent, they have the option of asking that car to come back out of stage and start the procedure again. Alternatively, the starter may ask you to come into stage ready to start the race if they believe that either the opponent has accidentally rolled through too far or that there has been no unfair advantage gained. You should comply with this instruction and either courtesy stage with the opponent if they have been pulled back, or go into stage as normal if asked to come forwards. The seven second rule only comes in to force if both cars were in pre stage. If you were not in the pre stage beams when the opposing stage bulbs come on, this is a matter for the starter. Do not be rushed, remain calm and give the control of the situation to the officials. Never allow an opponent to bully you into making mistakes. Drag racing is a courteous and friendly sport and should always remain so.

Troubleshooting

It is inevitable that at some stage in your career you are going to come across an issue with your car, or with racing that will have you scratching your heads in wonder at the ability of such a simple machine as a Junior Dragster to confound and confuse even the best engineers. The following are a collection of real occurrences. Some may seem ridiculous, but I promise they have all happened. Hopefully the lesson is plain. Always go back to simple basics and work forwards from there. Ruling issues out is the most important step on the route to solving the final problem.

The case of the car that wouldn't run.

At a three day event, a competitor went through each qualifying round on day one and the first round on day 2. After a short delay for a track clean up, the class was called to the pairing lanes again. One young man's car would not start for the warm up. This particular team were new to racing and had only just purchased the car, but they were pitted with a team that claimed to be experts who were helping fix the problem. All offers of help from other teams were turned down, the "experts" knew everything and didn't need any help, yet it seemed that the car would just not fire at all. The team missed the next qualifier and started asking around for parts. Their "expert" help had identified that the problem was due to a faulty fuel pump. A fellow team were carrying a spare and this was hastily fitted before the next qualifying round. Still the car refused to start. They tested the replacement pump to find that this one too was not working, no fuel was flowing, it had to be down to a problem with the compression meaning that the pressure pulse was too weak to pump the fuel. This was going to be a tough job to fix. Interested and helpful parents began to gather in the team's pit to help with the engine rebuild that would inevitably be needed. By now the "experts" had the head, side cover, carb and manifold off revealing a fully intact piston. The team were upset and looking on in horror as their engine, and weekend of racing both looked to be in serious doubt, it was at this point that someone drew their attention to the fact that the fuel tap was turned off! A great deal of time, effort and embarrassment could have been avoided if they had just gone back to absolute basics. Always check the fuel is switched on!

The case of the mixed messages

This one happened to me! Junior Dragster were called to the pairing lanes for a qualifying round. As usual, within minutes of the call, teams were starting engines all around us. Myself and my son were running through our pre-race jobs, checking tyre pressures, fuel, oil etc. My son shouted across the pit and what I heard was "I have topped up the fuel"; Unfortunately what he shouted was "have you topped up the fuel?" In all the noise, I just nodded. And so it was that we pushed to the pairing lanes, started the car and drove onto the track only for the car to die just after the bleach box. It had totally run out of fuel. If it was your job to do, make sure it was done, if it was someone else's job to do, make sure it was done!

The case of the car that wouldn't race

A team raced in Q1 and Q2 without any problems. In Q3 the car drove to the line without issue, but at the launch it died instantly. Having pushed back to the pits the team looked at the car and started it up again without any problems there did not seem to be any particular reason why it had died, so they got ready for Q4. Again, the car drove under power to the line, but again at the launch it died without moving more than 10 feet. Once more they pushed back to the pit. Having decided this must be a carburation issue, they set about stripping, cleaning and rebuilding the carb. Part way through the process it was noticed that the fuel had an unusual odour.

The team had recently purchased a new drum of fuel from a fellow racer. Having checked the labelling on the drum, it was discovered that the fuel was actually brake cleaner which will burn in the engine enough to tick over but will not burn well enough to power the car.

The racer they had purchased it from had handed over the wrong drum in an honest error. Draining out the whole system and replacing the brake cleaner with Methanol resolved all issues and the racer was able to continue in competition without any further problems. Always check that the fuel is the correct fuel!

The case of the car that wouldn't rev

A racer noticed a problem on a qualifying lap which was severely slowing the car down towards the end of the track. The driver managed to drive off the track safely, but the engine was struggling to stay running. Back at the pit the team started to chase every possible issue, stripping off the body and replacing wires to kill switches, flushing fuel tanks, changing fuel pumps etc. Nothing seemed to cure the problem. The team asked us to see if we could help. When we took the carb off the culprit became obvious. The team had not drained down or flushed out the carb between events and they were suffering from "the white death". This occurs to methanol cars when they are stored for more than a few days with methanol in the carburettor and fuel system. The methanol evaporates and leaves a white, semi-crystalline deposit in the jets and float bowl. This hampers carburettor operation enough to mean that cars cannot effectively run on full throttle. The carb was removed, stripped and thoroughly cleaned before reassembly. Once this was done, the car ran happily for the rest of the weekend. Always make sure you maintain your car!

The case of the car that wouldn't leave

A junior stock car made it through a round of eliminations at a full event which included pro classes. The track was fully prepped to take top fuel and the day was hot and sunny. The junior stock car made it round to the start line and drove into pre stage. When the car in the other lane moved forwards into stage the junior stock failed to come forwards. No amount of prompting from the track crew or the parents could make the car move up to the start line. Eventually the starter had no choice but to run the timing system and time out the poor youngster in the stock car.

When asked what had happened the team stated that the car was stuck to the track and lacked enough power to pull forwards. The driver was too frightened to press the pedal hard for fear of rolling through and risking an LB3A (Left Before Tree Activated) penalty.

Further questioning revealed that this team were using very low tyre pressures. As they thought that was what they ought to do because their "buddy" (A JMA crew chief) told them that his car ran tyre pressures of around 5psi. As discussed earlier in the book, tyre pressures for Junior Stock cars should be higher than those for Modified or Modified advanced cars. DO not believe that what is right for another team is right for you!

The case of the chain snapping car

A junior modified car had some work done to it over the closed season. At the first available test day they appeared and ran a couple of laps before snapping the chain. A second test day resulted in the same problem. When the competitive season commenced, the car would run no more than two laps before it snapped another chain.

The crew chief had bought industrial quantities of drive chains and was changing them on a seriously regular basis. Other crew chiefs kept offering to look at the car, but he was insistent that there was nothing wrong and it was "just the way this car is". Finally he allowed one of the other parents to look at it and discovered that the axle was ¼" out of line and the chain gears were a further ½" out of line. A few minutes with the correct tools and a good straight edge and the problems were resolved, the car didn't snap a chain ever again.

One off breakages are part of racing, continuous breakages indicate there is something else wrong. Do not let pride get in the way of engineering logic!

The case of the car that couldn't race

This particular incident happened to a friend whose son (nearly ten years later) has just about got over it! In a big season ending competition, the driver concerned was leading the championship at the last race of the season. He had qualified well and was through the first three rounds of competition. A win in the next round would mean he would mathematically win the championship regardless of what his rivals could do. During a slight rain delay, the boy's father was showing off the car to a couple of spectators. He showed them the car and the race kit and let them take pictures of their child in the driver's seat. To do this, he removed the racers helmet, gloves and neck brace from the car. Sadly he did not put the neck brace back in. When the cars were called to race the driver and his father pushed the car down to the pairing lanes and began to get ready to race. Since this was the fourth round there were only two pairs of cars and the class ran through very quickly. The safety crew would (quite rightly) not allow the driver to race without a neck brace and there was no time to run back and get it. They therefore forfeited the race and with it their hopes of a championship win. To add insult to injury the car they were supposed to race broke just off the line. Always triple check that you have everything you need before you leave your pit.

The case of the engine that died

Having undergone a winter rebuild a car was re-assembled the day before the first race of the season. Topped up with fresh fuel and oil, the engine was started back at base before being loaded and towed to the track. The engine started ok and ran for a couple of minutes then cut out. Thinking nothing of it, the team drove off to the race meeting and set up their pit. The car was scrutineered and checked out fine. Back at the pit a second attempt to start the engine resulted in nothing. Every system on the car was checked, replaced, cleaned, tested and found to be working. The spark plug had a spark, the valve timing was exactly correct, the fuel pump was working, everything checked out fine. Different fuel was run through the car, the coil was changed, both kill switches were tested as was the full electrical circuit. Nothing seemed to be wrong anywhere, but this engine would not run. Then the crew chief realised that whilst there was fuel, compression, spark and exhaust, maybe these were not happening in the exact correct order or timing. When they checked the car again, they found that the flywheel had sheared its key and rotated on the crankshaft so that the spark was happening at the wrong time. The engine simply could not work like this. Twenty minutes later the flywheel had been removed, cleaned, lapped back onto the shaft and refitted with a new key and the engine ran like a dream. Always work on the problem from the basics upwards. If it has fuel, spark, compression and exhaust at the right times, it should run fine.

The case of the 330ft race car

A car that had previously been running just fine suddenly cut out at 330ft and coasted to a halt on the racing surface during qualification. The car was towed off the track by the fire crew and returned to its pit. The team worked on the car between rounds but could find nothing wrong. In the next qualifier, the car started and drove to the line, when the lights dropped it launched perfectly but again cut out at 330ft and coasted to a halt to be towed off the track again by the fire crew. The team were scratching their heads looking for a solution. Fuel starvation seemed the obvious culprit so the fuel pump was changed. The car ran happily in the pit for several minutes, but in the next qualification round, exactly the same thing happened. No-one could come up with a solution or a reason. Overnight the team checked, cleaned, replaced or tested every component they could The next day in the first round of eliminations, the car did exactly the same thing, at 330ft it cut out and had to be retrieved from the track. The bewildered team packed up their race car and went home. The crew chief then tells of a random encounter with a motorcycle race mechanic and tuner who, when told what the issue was, correctly named the carburettor model without even seeing it. The mechanic had been crewing for a famous racer at the Isle of Man TT races on a bike equipped with four of these carburettors where an intermittent problem had been noted with cylinder 3 which looked like fuel starvation during the race, but could not be traced or replicated at the pit or in the workshop. Through rigorous and time consuming testing (probably only available to pro race teams) the cause had finally been identified. The main jet needle in these carburettors is mounted to the back of the slide by a small spring clip called an E clip. This can be attached to the needle in any of five or seven grooves which allow tuners to make the carb run richer or leaner at full throttle. If the E clip is worn, under heavy vibration it can release the needle at full throttle causing it to drop down and close the jet, thus cutting the fuel supply to the engine and causing it to stop. When the throttle is closed again the slide returns to the bottom of its travel and the needle follows its guide back to its original position when it pops back into the E clip as though it was never separated. When the engine gets back to the pit or workshop it is as though nothing ever happened. A new E clip (a few pennies worth of part) resolved the issue. You never know where the solution might come from, so take advantage of any knowledge you can.

Printed in Great Britain
by Amazon